Experiences
of an Inexperienced God

By
Tammara Or Slilat

PARTRIDGE

A Penguin Random House Company

To order additional copies of this book, contact
Toll Free 800 101 2657 (Singapore)
Toll Free 1 800 81 7340 (Malaysia)
orders.singapore@partridgepublishing.com

www.partridgepublishing.com/singapore

This book is dedicated to:

- My mother, Sim, who doesn't cease to marvel at my ingenuity in coming up with such fantastic nonsense;
- My father, Ram, who thinks that God having a wonderful sense of humor is information of the utmost importance to human kind;
- My son, Ori, who is always with me in spirit;
- My eldest daughter, Jasmin, who did neither cower nor blink before reading my lengthy poems and giving me her feedback;
- My youngest daughter, Shira, who listened patiently, contributed her opinion and in the end said that God is cool;
- Roi, who listened eagerly, made some good suggestions and helped me shape new words like "polylocational";
- Livna Seeon, who channeled the prologue straight from source;
- And finally a bouquet of freshly picked thanks to my Creator/s who made it all possible – I couldn't have done it without you.

Tammara Or Slilat   Arbel

1/1/11

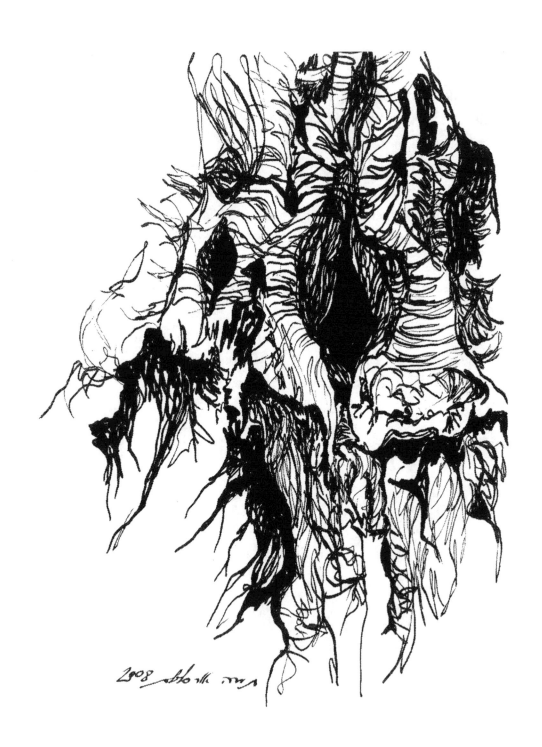

Boundless, soundless, absolutely

still

timeless, eventless,

a dream not yet awake,

shrouded in nothingness that knows

no reason, no purpose.

Is there an

I?

              found a

              singularity.

Did it drop through

itself from another universe?

Slippery along its event horizon, it was

a fixed splinter

in the undisturbed lumipresence.

Let it lie for a while

until curiosity suggested:

pour awareness into it. The initial shock

spelled: bad idea.

Densely dark

    inside -

crippled, cringed, compressed

so unlike

the mild translucent darkness of open space.

Then, in the beginning

of regret, found this guide -

The Abridged Manual of Godding

Bored of eternally talking to yourself? Tired of floating endlessly in the void, filled to the brim with your omnipresence? If you answered in the affirmative, consider becoming a God: mind expanding challenges guaranteed, twists and turns to the original plot as your creatures develop awareness and free will… Sure, the care-taking chores never end, but what else have you got to do with your time?

(From the back cover of the Manual)

New thoughts started

               murmuring, begetting shape -

do it (?) become a Creator (!)

make this universe opulent in colors

and intricate designs, boundless

abundance of life forms

constantly born, reborn,

               a dream within a dream,

the dreamer and the dream

co-creating a never-ending story,

an adventure, a mystery,

no being knows

how it ends, the wheres and the whens

The creatures will have free will,

reinvent themselves anew

every day

bequeath their experiences,

their tears of sorrow and joy

shall be drunk, life and death

experienced with each and everyone,

until once again all becomes one.

If you answered in the affirmative, follow the sequence below and get ready for the rockiest
ride of your life. However, if you choose not to become a Creator, please retract your presence
carefully and leave the way you came in.
(The Manual, 1.01)

Suddenly, on the outskirts of sensitivity
an internal stirring
began, expanding in all 12 dimensions,
gathering speed.

The miniscule specks of matter, once energized, started dancing,
warped into existence, away,
into and around them, the tiny explosions exponentially growing
it felt
sparkly, fuzzily bubbly, and

I, a ball of liquid black fire
quivering with unexplored potentials
on the verge
of yearning
to become

Before you begin, you must first establish the basic frequency of your newly-born universe. Would it be a universe of perfect harmony? Perhaps a universe of ties and control? The options are innumerable. To the beginner God we recommend the beautiful frequency of love. Though not the easiest one to work with, due to its volatile nature, its greatest advantage is its willingness to accept change, i.e. you can always correct your mistakes.

(The Manual, 1.02)

I thought I knew love: warm, tingling,
slowly filling up the cracks
in the vessels of light, holding tight.

I wanted to know love: the flux, the flow,
the highs, the lows, a sudden smile
unravels umbilical cords of light, holding tight.

Once you've reached maximum capacity, just melt down and let go… you'll feel de-pressured all at once, much relieved and extremely spacious.

(The Manual, 1.03)

In the beginning
a burning mass of pure longing, the closest
I've ever come to being solid, then
surrendered myself to the charged momentum
and the Big Release – the closest I've ever come
to the orgasm of living and dying –

In the beginning and in the end, everything is energy, which by itself is but a slower, much more

condensed expression of divine consciousness.

(The Manual, 1.04)

Matter is trapped Light.
Fast flown
            and straight ahead
until it's forced to fold upon itself,
the electrons' windmills turning, churning
in the cosmic wind, creating the grand illusion.

        Infinite Spirit contained, becomes Flesh and Blood.

                  Know
            that time,   time is circular,
        the transient -   eternal,
       only   constant, never
      changes,   in
     the beginning,   the end,
     matter –   molded, grasped,
     poked,   pierced, torn
      mended,   exalted,
        wretched,   matter is
         light, incarcerated

As a beginner god, you would probably want to use the technique known as Thought Creation.

For that you'll need words.

(The Manual, 1.06)

Like all great endeavors yet to come,

the Great Pyramid, the Crystal Temple,

the Theory of Relativity or Warp Drive spaceships,

    thought creation

   begins by catching

      one

      small

      word.

Words, in their pre-lingual phase, are abstract life forms that tend to swim in schools.
(The Manual, 1.09)

Unspoken,

    devoid of

        meaning, an empty

            shell floating

                  unaware up

            and down

          the cosmic

      plasma currents,

  sometimes

caught in a swirl

  of a solar wind, it dances

      a momentary minuet

         with other tadpole words.

            Meeting and parting, turning

           round, rising and falling,

        not a sound

      is heard, yet

     the music

   is recorded

  in kaleidoscopic

maneuvers,

    frozen

        silvery

            flakes

                flying

        to the beat

of a silent drum.

Words are needed in order to establish the infrastructure of concepts in your universe. The problem is you must catch them first. Though catching the first one is relatively easy, they immediately warn each other. So brace yourself, it's going to be quite a chase.

(The Manual, 1.11)

A flake of snow on your face
melts before you touch it,
a flake of word in your space
withers before you watch it,
its life span shorter than a quark's.

I must be patient. Track it down
through the storm, through the buzzing curve
of flashing, sardine-like words, never losing sight.

        Focus.

      Nothing else

         exists

         in the

          Now

        but that

      shy shifty shape,

    that fleeting floating flake.

Since words in their pre-lingual state are only two dimensional objects, it's clear why injecting them with meaning requires the delicate touch of a brain surgeon. The chosen frequency of energy must be carefully inserted inside the shell before it sets.

(The Manual, 1.13)

With infinite patience
I stroked its infinitesimal skin
pretending to be an experienced lover,
cajoled it to find
the exact point of entry
while flick-flacking backwards in free fall.

Remember that concepts vibrate in a wide range of frequencies. Sometimes they happen to overlap, so better keep the fundamental ones as short as possible, God being the shortest of them all.

(The Manual, 1.15)

Plato will be erroneously right.
Ideas aren't warmer or rougher
to the touch, nobler or purer than
the wonder-full creatures that will breathe, breed
and dream my universe into existence.
He, who would be accused of star-gazing,
cloud-herding, would have enjoyed watching
this. See how

the luminescent
cob-webs of energy coil, weave themselves
around an empty   c e n t e r, a giant cocoon waiting
for its embryo to manifest itself through their
love, their commitment. So shall I
create Human.

Although technically, it doesn't matter where you start poking your pins in the vast semantic field, choosing the firstborn word is critical, since that single word will determine the course of energy in your universe.

(The Manual, 1.17)

Light is good.

It launches a host

of beautiful fireflies:

radiance, luminescence,

shine, sparkle and glow,

scintillation, elucidation,

expose, disclose and throw

light on every conceivable object.

It makes you aware, it helps you beware

the darkened corners of obscurities.

Matter, placed in the center, branches out in four directions –

Wind

Water   Fire

Earth

Voicing the inserted intention is obviously the trickiest part, since no organ of speech has come

into existence, yet.

(The Manual, 1.21)

I was a mere babe playing
with my 'Build a Universe' kit.
A millennium had been spent
pondering over the problem of voicing.
Finally a solution dawned
on my fetal god consciousness.
A great vacuum was created by
withdrawing my divine awareness,
then a gust of wind
gushed into it whispering
the first word: Light.

Slowly,
stalactite formation
slow, light
gathered, turning from deep velvety
purple to hazel white
while darkness trickled
into huge ponds
of silence.

The ephemeral nature of the tiniest particles which enables them to exist in a few places at once,

can form the basis for the stabilization of solid energy.

(The Manual, 1.87)

A sticky cloud of polylocational particles
coming and going, zigzagging
across the threshold of reality,
and that makes stable and solid!
It was amusing, for a while, but
when I wanted to try something else,
the particles just kept on popping
and disappearing enthusiastically,
obviously expecting me to watch.

So I kept it - a particles' gig.
I hope someday someone will applaud them.
I know they would like that.

The energy in null is bipolar, based on one principle.

(The Manual, 1.90)

Energy poised
in perfect balance,
as an acrobat walking
the tight rope. Absolutely still,
you mustn't blink in the face
of the abyss, but glide
gracefully above it, giving
the impression of an effortless stride.

Or like a rope-pulling contest,
both parties equal in strength.
Muscles swelling, heels digging,
the rope - a humming violin cord.
As long as the balance is maintained, both ends
seem constant and consistent.

Matter is a tricky substance to work with. You may find that you have to allow yourself a few unsuccessful experiments before you get the hang of it.

(The Manual, 2.03)

A clump of Earth and a stretch of Sky -
together and apart, my first piece of art.

Earth lay purring. Her soft magenta surface
rising and falling rhythmically
while Sky drew her name in ultramarine clouds
on his white skin. Earth rolled idly,
to let Sky stretch himself over and around her,
as he poked spiral turquoise tunnels in her rosy flesh.

I watched their spacey dance,
their streaming, hypnotizing movements.
A clump of Earth and a stretch of Sky -
together and apart, my first piece of art.
Alas, to proceed I had to bring on
the Great Divide.
Little did I understand Separation.

Sky looked down lamenting
the distance from his beloved.

Days turned to years

and the cavities of Earth were soon filled

with his salty tears.

Earth swelled up towards Sky, bellowing huge

mountains that climbed on top of each other,

trying to touch, once more, her unreachable love.

The pandemonium was deafening.

I was delighted. Giant cobalt serpents seared

through Sky, ripping him apart.

Trying to explode himself back into oblivion

he only succeeded in making

thundering booms. I was elated.

Little did I understand Pain.

A clump of Earth and a stretch of Sky -

together and apart, my first piece of art.

Considering the magnanimity of the work and the intricate complexities involved, one thing is

certain: You're bound to make mistakes.

(The Manual, 2.88)

I cannot deny that

sometimes,

on several occasions actually

there were,

or rather, was

a doubt

whether

certain choices

were not

the most ideal

decisions

in the given

circumstances

of conflicting tendencies.

But the fabric of the universe

is unevenly woven, beautified by mistakes.

The disruption of flow

new patterns, new images creates.

Honestly, not in every situation

have I taken the ideal course of action.

Take the Flood - What was I thinking?

Millions of years of hard work

down the drain, drowned in rain,

and all because I didn't like the speed

with which the culture was developing,

thought they should spend more time working the land

instead of leaping fast-forward

to sipping Beaujolais in skyscrapers.

But the fabric of the universe

is unevenly woven, beautified by mistakes.

The disruption of flow

new patterns, new images creates.

Careful consideration should be given to the question of an energy source for your world that would enable the creation of biological life forms. The standard model is that of a star surrounded by planets… if you have an horticultural inclination, the use of a hydrogen-helium nuclear fusion yellow star is recommended.

(The Manual, 3.01)

Though forewarned, I did experiment
with purple, red and bright green suns.
The red ones were too weak and slow,
the purple burned hot and bright,
producing crystallized plants that glowed
in the deep velvety night.
The bright green ones were pretty, but still
not warm enough for the delicate flora I had in mind,
so finally I tried the yellow sun.
I blew up a thousand supernovas to create
the most beautiful one – Sol, queen of the solar system,
hidden in a curve in the Orion constellation,
a tiny speck of the Milky Way, one of the minor galaxies
of the 12th bubble in the local cluster of manifold universe.

The suns, transducers of bursting life force, spreading light, heat, intention and consciousness, function as powerful relay stations for sub-matter transmissions from the main singularity at the heart of the galaxy. They receive and transmit sub-matter rays that move intact through dense matter. These rays are hindered by neither space nor time. Sub-matter rays are the carriers of spiritual intention that lies at the heart of all created things, endowing them with meaning and purpose.

…

Life-force moves in sub-matter but cannot be converted to light, energy and matter without the presence of a transducer.

(The Manual, 3.22)

Metamorphosis – how fascinating:
Intention turns to creation
through sub-matter to force of life,
life-force to light, light to energy,
energy to matter and back again –
matter to energy, energy to light,
light to life-force, transmitted through sub-matter
returns information to intention.
As more and more creators-transducers of life-force
join in, we expand the boundaries of impossibility,
exploring the event horizon of reality.

That was the plan, but I

learned the hard way: how important

to keep pace, the multi-frequency metronome

beats relentlessly, a million orchestras play

together - or else watch worlds unseamed;

to instill clarity, leave no place

for ambiguities - or else watch

interstellar worms burrow through

the folds of space-time continuity;

to give instructions compatible with current space;

not to expect too much

of myself; not to berate

mine or any other self for failing

to live up to those expectations.

Beginning creators ask for

the tolerance of their creations.

The magnanimity of the work requires the application of complex multi-vibrational thought patterns elongated to strings.

(The Manual, 4.01)

Behold, my universe is harped

into existence. I start with

a silenced picked arpeggio, each string

lighting up, sustained

in the moment of enclosed creation.

Harmonized gently, the overtones reverberate

in subatomic spaces; then let the strumming begin –

I sweep the scales, slap the strings,

glide up and down, sliding and bouncing,

building thought forms that run

in all directions, all dimensions, rooting

newly born concepts of earth and flora

in the lower, slower humming cords,

then shooting up to the higher, finer

strings of the angelic realms that hum so fast

they are melted into light.

As the capsules in which physical beings are created, thought formations maintain the integrity of their material beings. It is vital to ascertain they are perfect in every aspect before embarking on physical creation itself.

(The Manual, 5.05)

The void is   pregnant with
    thought-forms,   matter poured
      into their cavities,   shaped in their
          image.

A flawed thought
    would   not
  sustain   matter
but dis in teg rate ir re vo cab ly

Intelligent creatures… though not an absolute must, are a great source of amusement. Remember, a Creator is defined by the creatures it gives life to, much as its creatures are defined by their own creations - their feelings, thoughts and deeds.

(The Manual, 6.01)

Intelligent beings discover each other, wrapped
in a fragile biological bubble they play
hide and seek among
the complementing opposites:
light and dark, matter and spirit,
good and evil, male and female -
the endless dance
of dualities attracted by love:
as below, so above.

Miniscule pieces of awareness racing past
each other in the dark, forming
everlasting, everchanging
relationships, moving in
predicted orbits round a central
sun held fast by love:
as below, so above.

Radiant, powerful beings,

striving to overcome

their self-imposed impediments,

aspiring to become

the creators they are, transducers

of energy operated by love:

as below, so above.

Thought-creation only seems difficult but it's actually quite easy once you've learned to hush all the residual noise. However, you should consider installing a time lag for your own creatures' thought-creation process. It's a recommended precaution against all sorts of mishaps that may occur as a result of their inexperience, irresponsibility or lack of discipline.

(The Manual, 6.05)

The Time Lag: Postpone installment.

We are curious to see what our creatures are capable of.

Construct a frame of mind

for the chosen male and female prototypes:

tell them a certain tree, randomly chosen, is the key

to their mental evolution.

To ensure the strongest incentive for action,

tell them NOT to eat of its fruit.

…

Of all the trees in the garden that legless reptile

has chosen the marked tree to take its nap on.

I hope it doesn't scare her away. Hush –

here she comes, glancing sideways.

…

Fascinating: By the sheer power of her own conviction

she has transformed that plain fruit

into a mind-evolving enhancer for her and her mate.

Soon they'll elevate themselves from beasts to human beings.

…

Progress: The creatures developed self awareness

and social consciousness – they started making clothes.

We're proud of them, such a fine pair:

She is the inquisitive entrepreneur

and what he lacks in imagination he complements

with ready muscle power and stamina.

…

Problem: Life in Eden – apparently too comfortable.

They're torpid now, indulging their acedia. It saddens us

to see they even relinquished the great taxonomy

of all the wonderful creatures we made.

…

Solution: Banish them from Easy Street,

make them face some real challenges,

jump-start their evolution.

Before embarking on the massive project of creating intelligent creatures, you should consider whether to make them sentient or not. Insentient beings are predictable and easier to handle, whereas sentient beings are by far more complex and erratic, thus making the development of your universe precarious in nature...

In case you've chosen to take the risk of creating beings who are in full emotional capacity, you should be forewarned to carry out the process of creation with the utmost care and deliberation. Do not install big evolutionary jumps but rather take the slow course of random mutations with occasional corrections in order to ensure mature emotional control for your creatures, preferably before they reach a destructive technological level. Bear in mind that emotions are highly explosive, making sentient beings volatile in nature.

(The Manual 6.10)

My thoughts reeled, weaving fantastic shapes:
agony manufactured liquid compound for the release of toxins;
beacons of light ignited by intense pleasure;
the ripple effect of the lighter energies vibrating through
all bodies; the excruciation of disconnection.
I wanted to try them all, taste each and every one...
So, orderly and boring or unexpected and fun?

Most of the universe will be on safe mode, but

on one planet, one species will be

the Jumping Jack in my Universe Box,

the Trickster with the power to elevate all, or end the game,

for theirs alone will be the freedom of choice.

All is foreseen and permission granted:

let the Great Game begin.

In order to research a certain emotion it is advisable to project its opposite emotion. The contrast between them is often more revealing than the experienced emotion itself.
(The Manual, 6.19)

Love feels fuzzy and warm,
but for an in-depth study its opposites
are needed: hate, cruelty, indifference.
Once I create the frequency
of love, the whole emotional spectrum
will be laid out as a peacock's tail:

for Hate - reverse the poles.
It's but a mirror image of Love.
Cruelty is enhanced Indifference,
to get Indifference - withdraw Love.
Jealousy is self-love with a twist
at the core that perpetuates
the need, instead of its fulfillment.
Anger and Vengeance are fear-based
emotions. Fear is easily created
by experiencing loss of Love.

The lighter emotions are the easiest – Joy, Happiness

and Laughter are but slight variations of the main frequency

and need only a little fine-tuning

with different accentuation.

O, I thought I was so clever… manipulating

the polarity to create all those highly charged potentials

like a balloon twister in kids' parties,

pulling out once a rabbit and once a dog.

O, I thought I was so clever… yearning

to experience all those new, exciting emotions

I've engineered, ornamented Pandora boxes

waiting

Different emotions produce different effects. Examine the outcome carefully before making

your final decision as to the nature of the effect.

(The Manual, 6.67)

This was the real gift of the random tree

that became known as the Tree of Knowledge:

to sense, to feel, to know

Pain, Anxiety and Fear,

for our creatures are grand, formidable,

created in our likeness, they deserve

a worthy challenge:

to walk barefoot on burning coals,

trusting in Love, believing

in their ability

to overcome, prevail, remain open-eyed

and in spite of everything –

rejoice,

      create,

           love

I did

not comprehend

the full extent,

I did not

know how hard, how

Fear - the jagged brim

of a metal can, only a light stroke

can survive its touch, radiating electric thorns –

Tzink, Tzink, it sets ablaze adjacent halo fields.

Pain – the cold fire, allegedly non-consuming, just

gnawing through the core as a pour of liquid nitrogen,

while the crust remains whole – slowly accumulates,

white ash in the corners of eyes.

Anxiety – the dense woolen blanket

blocking air and light –

folds the time-space continuity into a black hole.

but

the

imaginary

snake in

the garden

and the woman

supposedly coaxing,

seducing, (man comfortably

rendered guilt-free), belittled, twisted and

turned the original lesson

yet

the challenge remains the same:

walk barefoot on burning coals while trusting

in Love, believe in your ability

to overcome,

prevail,

remain

open-eyed,

in spite of

everything –

rejoice, create, love

Due to the dimensional shift in the transition from pure consciousness to energy and the compression of that energy into matter, every creation would be slightly warped. As a result, all your creatures should be equipped with a warped perception of reality in order to perceive it correctly.

(The Manual, 6.77)

Like playing hide and seek in a carnival
of funny mirrors.
Warped to Perfection.
Will the deviation
from harmony be considered flawed,
or would it define
another kind of beauty?

For the fabric of the universe
is unevenly woven, beautified by mistakes.
The disruption of flow
new patterns, new images creates.

The illusion of a linear timeline is an essential prerequisite to the evolution of your creatures.

Without it they would have no incentive for spiritual development and growth.

(The Manual, 6.82)

They will march, our little soldiers of destiny,

to the beat of the unbeatable drum - time

measured by slow spinning, turning round,

burning their lives' wick,

quick, quick, in the great wheel of Samsara

all beings will be called to reflect upon: times

they renounced love, hearts

they closed, rivers of joy

they did not immerse in

When creating your creatures you should take into account the ripple effect on your own expanding awareness. You would have to go through a period of adjustment in which you would learn to perceive your created world through the accumulative tiny consciousnesses and limited perception of your creatures. Remember that due to the dimensional shift you will not have a direct access to your created world and you'd be able to work your influence only through the medium of your creatures.

(The Manual, 6.90)

I understand now, how
it feels to have a fly-like vision times trillions,
a kaleidoscope of perceptions, innumerable sensory organs,
from microscopic membranes to the surface of a star,
from the slowly accumulated, decade span perception of stones
to the flashing firefly split crack of bacteria,
infinite adjacent energy fields, co-fluxing, co-merging,
        I'm at the heart of each and every one
        I'm all and I'm none.

Epilogue: *To my creatures*

I that is not an I yet
holds out a hand that is not a hand,
calling my creatures to approach
the intimacy of deep serenity.
Take a bow to yourselves,
for being here,
for life, for the different,
for eternity present
for the fold in time unfolding,
for the whole you cannot be,
whispers: I am you.

For everything I haven't
and will not be,
for the songs I haven't sung,
for the dances I will not dance,
for the seed sprouting
not knowing if it's going to meet rain
or sun biting dry, barren root;
for the doors I closed behind
moving forward,
for choosing each and every moment
eternal being me.

The light that is not light

lives within you.

The life that is not life

sings to you:

praise life, cheer life.

For that which

wishes to be born urges you:

wake up, breathe the breath of life into me.

This is my riddle, waiting for you to solve,

but until you cross the threshold you will not know.

Listen, heaven is calling you, come beyond the verge

of the impossible, know

that which you cannot understand,

take the hand you cannot hold,

approach the intimacy of deep serenity,

take a bow to yourselves,

for being here.

I don't deny

I wonder too

why you don't despise me

now you know I don't know

if it was worth it all.

But leaving judgment aside

we decide not to decide,

what matters is the life

that will be born out of us

hailing us, we are

the present.

We are heading towards

an unknown vision,

to know what is beyond

our imagination.

When overcome by hardship and sorrow

shall we say we're tired?

Shall we say enough?

When we're overwhelmed,

broken, bent,

who shall save

my lost children?

So between nothingness and empowerment

There's always a dose of modesty,

for I who wanted to escape myself

am cut from myself forever.

Life is not for me and I am not in it

but what am I without it?

And now and always

one more moment unknown

clutched between my fangs,

and I that is not an I yet,

so bare, forever slipping from my hands.